NATIONAL GEOGRAPHIC | **GLOBAL ISSUES**

MW00352511

CLIMATE
CHANGE

Andrew J. Milson, Ph.D.
Content Consultant
University of Texas at Arlington

Acknowledgments

Grateful acknowledgment is given to the authors, artists, photographers, museums, publishers, and agents for permission to reprint copyrighted material. Every effort has been made to secure the appropriate permission. If any omissions have been made or if corrections are required, please contact the Publisher.

Instructional Consultant: Christopher Johnson, Evanston, Illinois

Teacher Reviewer: Mary Trichel, Atascocita Middle School, Humble, Texas

Photographic Credits

Front Cover, Inside Front Cover, Title Page
©Ralph Lee Hopkins/National Geographic Stock. **4** (bg) ©Ralph Lee Hopkins/National Geographic Stock. **6** (bg) ©Barry Lewis/In Pictures/Corbis. **7** (tl) Precision Graphics. **8** (bg) Mapping Specialists. **10** (bg) ©REUTERS/Rodrigo Arias. **12** (t) ©Yann Arthus-Bertrand/Corbis. (cr) ©REUTERS/Carlos Duarte. **14** (bg) ©Gg/Gg Collection/age fotostock. **16** (bg) ©Stephen Frink/Photodisc/Getty Images. **17** (bl) Mapping Specialists. **18** (t) ©Luis Marden/National Geographic Stock. **20** (bg) ©WaterFrame/Alamy. (bl) ©Reinhard Dirscherl/Alamy. **22** (bg) ©Armin Rose/Alamy. (bl) ©Fiona Stewart/Oceans 8 Productions. **24** (t) ©Fiona Stewart/Oceans 8 Productions. (br) ©Ronald Karpilo/Alamy. **27** (t) ©AP Photo/Jennifer Knight. **28** (tr) ©Brand X Pictures/Jupiterimages. **30** (tr) ©Stephen Frink/Photodisc/Getty Images. (br) ©WaterFrame/Alamy. **31** (tr) ©Yann Arthus-Bertrand/Corbis. (bg) ©Don Farrall/Photodisc/Getty Images. (bl) ©Glen Allison/Photodisc/Getty Images. (br) ©Gg/Gg Collection/age fotostock.

For permission to use material from this text or product, submit all requests online at www.cengage.com/permissions

Further permissions questions can be emailed to permissionrequest@cengage.com

Visit National Geographic Learning online at www.NGSP.com.

Visit our corporate website at www.cengage.com.

Printed in the USA.

RR Donnelley, Jefferson City, MO

ISBN: 978-07362-97899

12 13 14 15 16 17 18 19 20 21

10 9 8 7 6 5 4 3 2 1

Earth's CHANGII CLIMATE

Pacific Realm
IN PERIL

The Republic of Palau consists of a group of low-lying atolls in the far-western portion of the Caroline Islands, which lie just north of the equator.

ADOPTING NEW PRACTICES

Guatemala is seeking ways to mitigate, or decrease, the impact of climate change. Some farmers have turned toward **sustainability**, land management that conserves the ecological balance and natural resources. For example, some farmers use organic fertilizers instead of chemicals that pollute water sources. Other farmers plant crops that can tolerate heavy rains or drought. In addition, many farmers adjust planting and harvesting times for greater yields. In these ways, growers are adapting to the new weather patterns resulting from climate change.

People are also learning to manage their forests better. In the Petén (PEE-tin) region of Guatemala, an environmental group teaches the community how to grow trees and harvest wood in a sustainable way. The wood is used to produce *xate* (ZAYT), a type of palm leaf used by florists, and *chiclé* (CHY-kuhl), used in chewing gum. Selling such products provides higher incomes for local people and protects the forests.

In Carmelita, the environmental group helps local people find international markets for wood products. If people benefit from selling wood, they will plant trees. This process, which is called reforestation, can help lessen the effects of climate change.

WORKING TOGETHER

Guatemala is ranked as one of 10 countries worldwide most vulnerable to climate change. It has joined a coalition of countries seeking help from wealthier developed countries, which are largely responsible for greenhouse gas emissions. One program works to reduce annual CO_2 levels equal to the emissions of 145,000 cars. By working together, Guatemalans hope to restore and preserve natural resources for future generations.

Explore the Issue

1. **Analyze Problems** How is climate change affecting Guatemala?

2. **Analyze Solutions** How can countries work together to reduce the effects of climate change?

Some Guatemalan farmers use organic fertilizers to sustain the health of the soil and water table. The market for organic crops is growing. Many people choose only pesticide-free foods from grocers and restaurants.

On this Guatemalan mountainside, cropland has replaced forests. As a result, the land is more vulnerable to climate change.

GUATEMALA'S DISAPPEARING FORESTS

While not heavily industrialized, Guatemala contributes to global warming in other ways. Each year the world loses forests through **deforestation**, the process of cutting down and clearing trees from land. Between 1990 and 2010, Guatemala lost almost 25 percent of its forests to commercial plantations. Other land was cleared for fuel or used to manufacture **biofuel**—a renewable energy source made from organic materials, such as plant and animal waste. Fewer trees remain to absorb harmful carbon dioxide and release beneficial oxygen.

Loss of forests leaves open land more vulnerable to strong storms. In flooding that followed Hurricane Stan, mudslides devastated small villages that lay below barren hillsides where trees had been cut down. In defiance of forest preservation laws, illegal logging operations still threaten the forests. When loggers burn the underbrush in drought conditions, fires can quickly burn out of control and destroy more trees.

> **"It rained for eight days, 24 hours per day. The rivers rose. In my village we lost 27 houses . . . We lost our entire crop."**
> —Efrain, a farmer, describes Hurricane Stan

CLIMATE AND CROPS

Climate change has already adversely affected Guatemala's growing season. In recent years, the spring rainy season has begun later in the year. This change has surprised farmers who have tilled the soil for many years. With a shortened growing season, their fields can no longer support two crops of corn. For some farmers, one harvest is not enough to support their families and livestock. Other crops suffer too. For example, without a dry spell in the midst of the rainy season, fungi can infect and kill tender coffee bean plants.

Not long ago, a record drought left hundreds of thousands hungry. The drought was made worse because of El Niño, a climate pattern of unusual warming of surface waters along the west coast of South America. During this pattern, climate cycles around the world are disrupted. To what extent the pattern is driven by global warming remains unclear.

During Hurricane Stan, a number of hillside hamlets and small villages were destroyed in mudslides. Many lives were lost.

A VULNERABLE PLACE

Farmers in Guadalupe (gwah-duh-LOOP), a village in Guatemala, feel the effects of climate change personally. On one small farm, the Transito (tran-ZEE-toh) family used to harvest about 26 sacks of corn each year. This filled the family's needs and left some to sell. In 2011, however, the family harvested only 5 sacks of corn, an 80 percent drop in yield. Heavy rains and hail had ruined the crop. In the previous two years, many farmers lost a percentage of their crops due to extreme weather events. As a result, some wait to plant crops later in the year in order to ensure the survival of the plants.

Unfortunately, scientists predict that longer periods of drought will alternate with heavy rainfall and flooding. In recent years, Guatemala has experienced more winter rain, later spring rains, and violent storms followed by drought. In 2009, the country experienced the longest dry spell in 30 years. A year later, the rainy season was the heaviest in 60 years.

IN HARM'S WAY

Guatemala also lies in the path of hurricanes, fierce tropical storms that form at sea. With winds above 74 miles per hour, the storms often drive heavy rain inland. Many scientists think that warmer ocean water is likely to increase the number and intensity of hurricanes in the future.

Three storms in the past 20 years—tropical storm Agatha (2010) and Hurricanes Stan (2005) and Mitch (1998)—caused extensive damage and loss of life in Guatemala. Hurricane Stan hit Guatemala's farmers hardest. The storm drove in heavy rains that lasted for several days, right before the harvest season. Fast-moving rivers of water washed out roads and flooded fields. Devastating mudslides destroyed homes and killed people and livestock.

If current weather changes continue, some scientists warn that rising sea levels and tropical storms will cause even more damage. Because this region is especially vulnerable to extreme weather events, Guatemala has become a vigilant and proactive partner with its neighbors to fight climate change.

GUATEMA
Adapts to Cha

Heavy rains from tropical storm Agatha caused a 330-foot-deep sinkhole in the middle of Guatemala City.

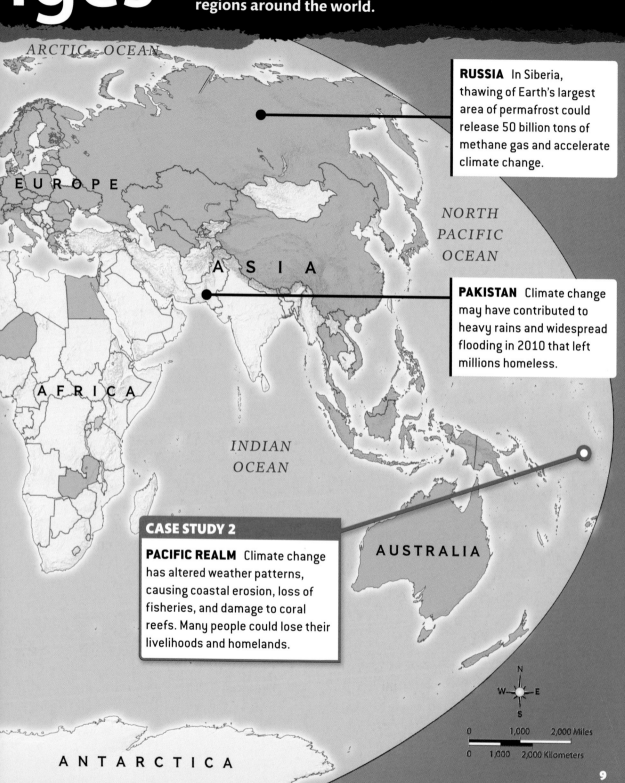

ARCTIC OCEAN

EUROPE

RUSSIA In Siberia, thawing of Earth's largest area of permafrost could release 50 billion tons of methane gas and accelerate climate change.

NORTH PACIFIC OCEAN

A S I A

PAKISTAN Climate change may have contributed to heavy rains and widespread flooding in 2010 that left millions homeless.

AFRICA

INDIAN OCEAN

CASE STUDY 2

PACIFIC REALM Climate change has altered weather patterns, causing coastal erosion, loss of fisheries, and damage to coral reefs. Many people could lose their livelihoods and homelands.

AUSTRALIA

| 0 | 1,000 | 2,000 Miles |
| 0 | 1,000 | 2,000 Kilometers |

ANTARCTICA

9

Climate Challe

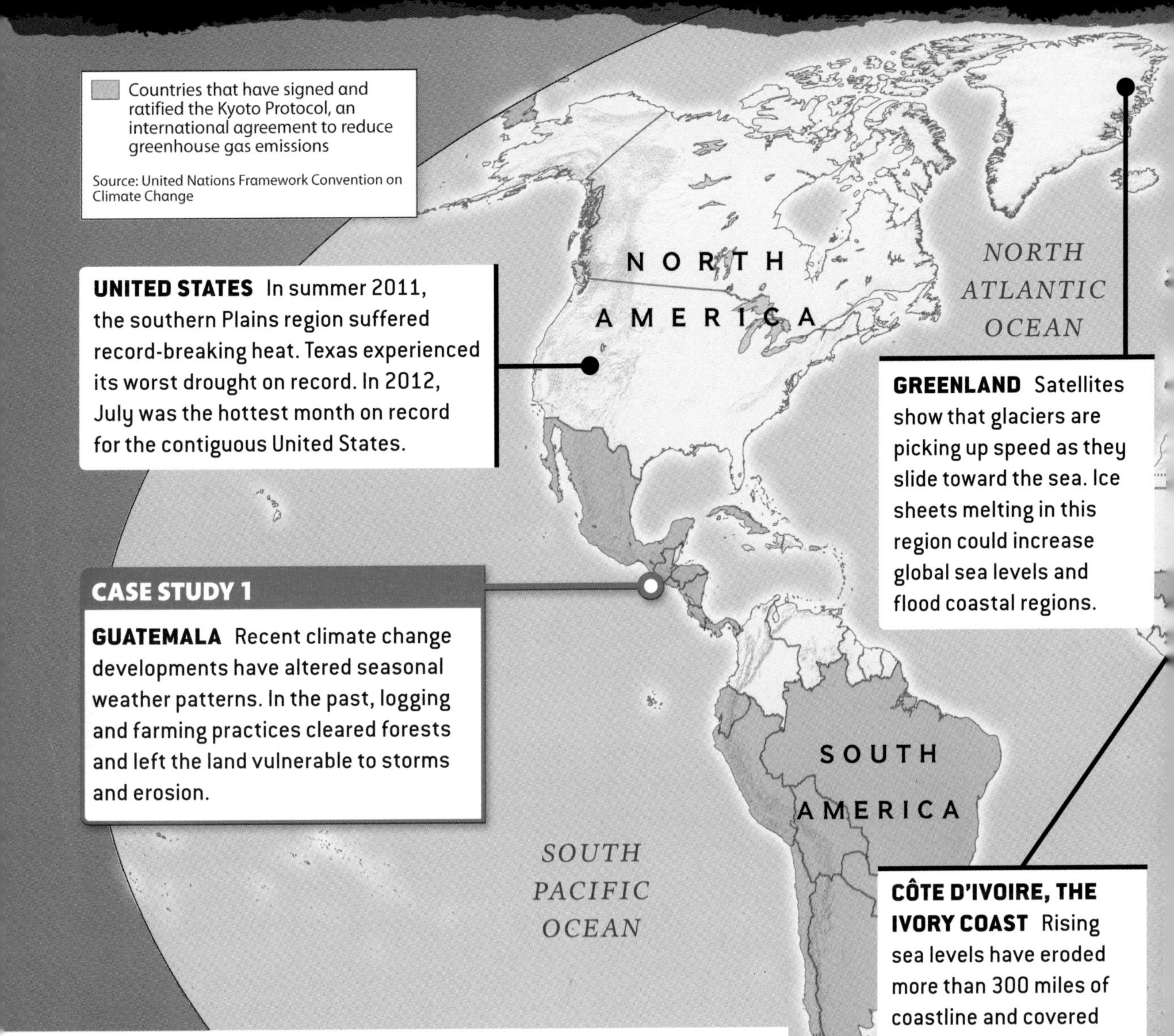

Countries that have signed and ratified the Kyoto Protocol, an international agreement to reduce greenhouse gas emissions

Source: United Nations Framework Convention on Climate Change

NORTH AMERICA

NORTH ATLANTIC OCEAN

UNITED STATES In summer 2011, the southern Plains region suffered record-breaking heat. Texas experienced its worst drought on record. In 2012, July was the hottest month on record for the contiguous United States.

GREENLAND Satellites show that glaciers are picking up speed as they slide toward the sea. Ice sheets melting in this region could increase global sea levels and flood coastal regions.

CASE STUDY 1

GUATEMALA Recent climate change developments have altered seasonal weather patterns. In the past, logging and farming practices cleared forests and left the land vulnerable to storms and erosion.

SOUTH AMERICA

SOUTH PACIFIC OCEAN

CÔTE D'IVOIRE, THE IVORY COAST Rising sea levels have eroded more than 300 miles of coastline and covered coral reefs in silt. In 2011, coastal homes in Abidjan were destroyed and several dozen families lost their homes.

Explore the Issue

1. **Interpret Maps** What kinds of extreme weather events were linked to climate change in the United States and Pakistan?

2. **Make Inferences** How might accelerated climate change in Greenland affect the Pacific Realm?

THE GREENHOUSE EFFECT

1. Radiation from the sun passes through Earth's atmosphere.
2. Some is absorbed and warms the surface.
3. Some is reflected back into space.
4. Some is trapped in Earth's atmosphere by a layer of greenhouse gases.
5. Some radiation is reflected back to Earth, where it increases surface temperatures.

Sun

3

1

2

4 Greenhouse Gases

Atmosphere

5

Earth

Source: National Oceanic and Atmospheric Administration

WHY IS EARTH WARMING?

Most scientists do not regard current climate change as part of a natural cycle. Instead, they believe that human activities, especially the burning of **fossil fuels**, cause or speed up global warming. Carbon-based fossil fuels, namely coal and oil, form in the earth from decaying plants and animals over millions of years. These fuels power electricity plants, industry, homes, and most forms of transportation.

Burning carbon-based fuels releases chemical compounds, or **greenhouse gases**, into the atmosphere where they trap solar heat near Earth's surface. A common greenhouse gas (GHG) is carbon dioxide (CO_2). Others include methane, nitrous oxide, and water vapor. Human activities have increased atmospheric CO_2 levels by one-third since the mid-1700s.

Many scientists want to limit GHG levels to no more than twice the levels during the 1800s. To reach this goal, current emissions would need to be cut by 50 to 80 percent. Scientists recommend developing alternative **renewable energy** sources, such as solar, wind, and geothermal and wind power. Unlike fossil fuels, these sources do not harm the environment.

Climate change affects different regions in different ways. The case studies illuminate changes in two different regions: Central America and the Pacific Realm.

Explore the Issue

1. **Analyze Causes** How do CO_2 emissions contribute to global warming?

2. **Analyze Effects** How does global warming affect Earth?

HOW DOES CLIMATE CHANGE AFFECT LIFE ON EARTH?

Polar bears make their homes far from people, in the frozen Arctic. Using sea ice as platforms, they stalk their main prey: seals. However, the polar bears' icy home is changing. The sea ice on which they depend is shrinking. What's the reason? The answer is **climate change**, which is a long-term change in the average weather conditions on Earth. The specific type of climate change is **global warming**, a rise in the average temperature near Earth's surface. Today's climate change affects more than just polar bears. It affects all life on Earth.

Arctic sea ice is forming later in the year and melting earlier. As a result, polar bears have a shorter hunting season. If sea ice continues to shrink, two-thirds of polar bears could disappear by 2050.

Over the past 100 years, Earth's average temperature has risen about 1.4° Fahrenheit. This may not seem like much, but this rise is having global effects. Changing weather patterns are causing wildlife habitats to disappear. Gradual warming of Earth's coldest regions is shrinking ice sheets and glaciers.

Although most scientists agree the planet is warming, some people deny it or disagree on *why* it's happening. Earth's climate has changed many times in the past. Is the current climate change part of a natural cycle, as some people claim?

In the United States, almost one-third of greenhouse gas emissions come from transportation vehicles, mostly cars.

SMALL ISLANDS FACE BIG CLIMATE THREATS

Chief Manno Pekaicheng (PEH-kay-cheng) of Ifalik Island worries about his people and his home. The **atoll**, or ring-shaped coral island on which he lives, lies in the tropical waters of the western Pacific Ocean. Ifalik is part of the Federated States of Micronesia (FSM), a string of islands that lie about three-quarters of the way from Hawaii to Indonesia. In 2008, islands in Micronesia experienced extremely high tides. The tides damaged homes, eroded coastal land, and flooded cropland with salt water. Chief Pekaicheng wonders if his people and island can survive the effects of climate change. As he puts it, "The big countries are contaminating the whole universe. And it's getting us before it gets them."

Many scientists believe that climate change is probably causing stronger storms and increasing risks of droughts and floods in the Pacific Realm region, which includes all the islands in the western Pacific Ocean. It is also causing sea levels to rise, a major threat to low-lying islands like many in the Federated States of Micronesia. If sea levels were to rise two feet or higher, inhabitants might be forced to evacuate some of the lowest islands, such as Kiribati (ki-rib-BAH-tee) and Tuvalu (too-VAH-loo). Higher islands could suffer severe damage to their coastal areas, where 80 percent of people live. Salt water flowing into **aquifers**, layers of underground rock that contain water, would pollute freshwater sources, making them unfit for drinking.

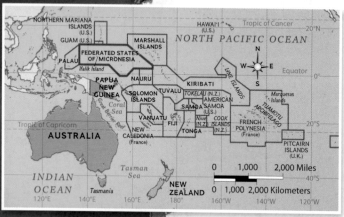

The Federated States of Micronesia consist of four major island groups of 607 islands with 100,000 inhabitants.

Like the countries in the Caribbean and Central America, the small islands of the Pacific Realm contribute little to greenhouse gas emissions. Yet these islands are feeling the effects of climate change. Pacific Islanders have lived in harmony with the ocean for centuries, but climate change now threatens their way of life. One scientist says, "Adaptation and survival that has developed over thousands of years now has to change overnight."

The people of Fiji cooperate to net fish. Rising sea levels due to climate change threaten their way of life.

DISRUPTING PEOPLE'S LIVES

Climate change affects where people live and how they make a living. In places such as Fiji (FEE-jee), even small rises in sea level mean higher tides and storm surges. Because the center of Fiji's main island is mountainous, it is not a safe place for evacuees if the coastal regions flood. In the event of evacuation, large numbers of islanders throughout the region might be forced to leave their homes for good.

Studies suggest that large areas of permafrost—the thick subsurface of frozen ground primarily found in polar regions—are melting faster than expected. As a result, methane emissions increase. In addition, global sea levels might rise higher than predicted. Some believe that the *El Niño* weather pattern increases sea levels.

Climate change is likely to make hurricanes stronger too. When they make landfall, the storms can devastate **infrastructure**—bridges, power plants, and public buildings. Rebuilding takes time and money, which is scarce in many island countries.

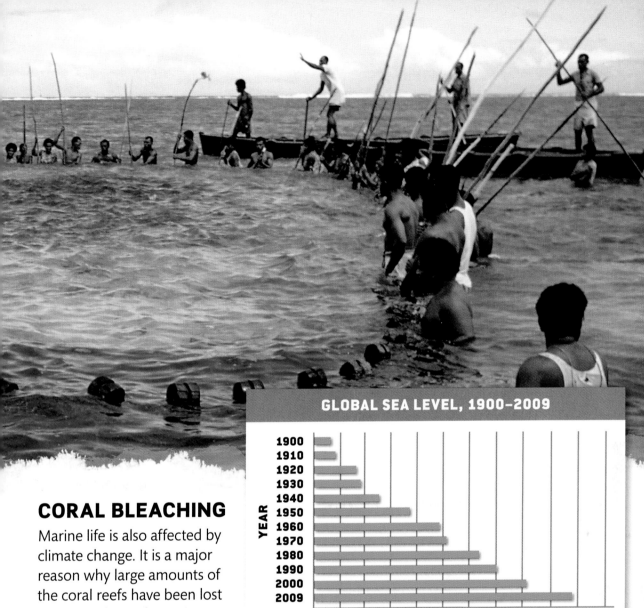

GLOBAL SEA LEVEL, 1900–2009

YEAR	
1900	
1910	
1920	
1930	
1940	
1950	
1960	
1970	
1980	
1990	
2000	
2009	

-140 -120 -100 -80 -60 -40 -20 0 20 40 60 80
SHOWN AS DIFFERENCE FROM 1990 (MILLIMETERS)

Source: CSIRO. Published by National Oceanic and Atmospheric Administration, 2009

CORAL BLEACHING

Marine life is also affected by climate change. It is a major reason why large amounts of the coral reefs have been lost in the Pacific Realm region since the 1980s. As carbon dioxide emissions increase, ocean temperatures rise and the water becomes more acidic. These conditions cause bleaching, which kills coral reefs. Stronger El Niño events, which most scientists think are due to climate change, make bleaching worse.

Thriving coral reefs support a variety of plants, fish, and other organisms. Fishing and tourist industries also depend on the reefs. Yet there is a delicate balance in the sea. Abundant fish actually help coral recover faster from bleaching by keeping the amount of algae near the reefs in balance. Therefore, overfishing near reefs can add to the problems of climate change.

In Raja Ampat, West Papua, Indonesia, an established mangrove stand helps stabilize the soil and prevent erosion.

Mature mangroves have large root systems that thrive above and below the water line. These unique trees prevent erosion, act as water filters, and provide habitat for shellfish and corals.

1.5 TO STAY ALIVE

Island countries are most vulnerable to climate change and have the fewest resources to deal with its effects. To increase global awareness of the climate threats they face, they formed an alliance. The Alliance of Small Island States (AOSIS) promotes its climate change goals with the slogan "1.5 to Stay Alive." In light of the fact that Earth's temperature has already risen 1.4° Fahrenheit, the alliance wants industrialized countries to take steps to limit the rise in average global temperature to 2.7° Fahrenheit (1.5° Celsius). The island countries think this goal will keep sea level rise from threatening their existence. A total of 80 countries throughout the world now support this goal.

The countries also want to reduce CO_2 emissions well below their current level in order to achieve this goal. Their target is more aggressive than the one proposed by industrialized countries that want more time to reduce emissions. Tonga, an island country in the Pacific Realm, wants to use more renewable energy. New Zealand is helping by providing funds for a large solar power plant there.

Another initiative is similar to reforestation. Australia is funding a program to plant **mangroves**—tropical saltwater plants that form dense masses of supporting roots—on Kiribati. Mangroves help prevent erosion along the coasts caused by rising sea levels and strong storms.

The small island countries have asked for financial and technical help to adapt to climate change. These countries want to develop more sustainable ways and decrease their use of fossil fuels. Larger countries, including the United States, have pledged financial support. United by location and a common threat, the small island countries hope to achieve their goals and preserve their homeland.

Explore the Issue

1. **Summarize** How is climate change affecting people who live in the Pacific Realm?

2. **Draw Conclusions** Why might small island countries and larger, more industrialized countries disagree on climate change goals?

Exploring Antarctic Ocean

Under sail to King George Island, Antarctica, explorer Jon Bowermaster crosses Drake Passage, one of the windiest places on Earth.

Towering icebergs rise above the ocean waters near the Antarctic Peninsula.

TAKING EARTH'S PULSE

Explorer Jon Bowermaster has seen the effects of climate change all over the world. Awarded grants by the National Geographic Expeditions Council, Bowermaster developed the Oceans 8 project in 1999. Since then, he has explored the oceans of the world and shared his work in documentary films and in articles in magazines such as *National Geographic*.

Bowermaster has led expeditions to all seven continents. He focused on oceans because they cover the majority of Earth's surface. The oceans actually form one vast sea with different names in different places. Covering more than 70 percent of Earth's surface, they absorb more than 80 percent of the heat trapped by greenhouse gases. Almost half the world's population depends on the oceans for food, transportation, and energy. Rising sea levels threaten billions of people around the world.

CHECKING EARTH'S HEALTH

Expeditions to the southernmost continent are limited by its extreme climate. During the long Antarctic winter, new ice doubles the surface area of the continent. This natural expansion provides a suitable habitat for penguins, seals, and seabirds but not for people. Thick ice sheets cover the continent year-round. So, explorers must wait for the short summer months to navigate the waters that surround the continent.

In January 2008, Bowermaster and his team set sail for West Antarctica. Just like the penguins in the region, the explorers quickly learned to navigate around icebergs that had broken off from **ice shelves**, massive platforms of ice that extend from the shore into the ocean. When floating chunks of ice collide, even large ships with reinforced hulls can become trapped in ice jams.

The team launched kayaks from the transport ship and paddled toward the peninsula. The feat required nerves of steel because floating ice can easily capsize lighter craft. As the team explored the waters surrounding West Antarctica, they found evidence of climate change. "If you believe as I do that Earth is a living thing, then Antarctica is its pulse," Bowermaster observes. Climate changes that occur on the most remote continent affect all life on Earth.

In light, maneuverable kayaks, Oceans 8 explorers paddle around floating icebergs off the Fish Islands, Antarctica.

STUDYING THE WATERS

In particular, Bowermaster believes that the waters around Antarctica are an important indicator of climate change. Although these waters contain only about 5 percent of the world's seawater, they provide a home for nearly 20 percent of its sea life. However, rising temperatures are changing the patterns of the waters' wildlife. Bowermaster noted not only a decline in the number of krill and Adélie penguins but also an increase in plant populations.

Human activity may also affect the region. Bowermaster and his team encountered a leopard seal asleep on a floating piece of ice and some rare white penguins on their expedition. However, they also observed a surprising number of tourist ships in the region—about 15. Bowermaster says that 10 or 12 years ago, "if you saw one private sailboat here it was amazing." Local scientists will monitor the impact of this increased tourism.

These photos of Muir Glacier in Alaska were taken 100 years apart. They show the effects of global warming in another part of the world.

> "If you believe as I do that Earth is a living thing, then Antarctica is its pulse." —Jon Bowermaster

KEEPING WATCH

As Bowermaster navigated Antarctica's ocean, he was surprised by the amount and thickness of the ice. During the previous winter, Antarctica had experienced colder than usual temperatures. Bowermaster fears that the thick ice may prompt people to question whether climate change in Antarctica is happening. He points out that the ice is due to seasonal weather and is not a sign that climate change isn't real.

In fact, Bowermaster learned that the continent needs to be watched closely. As he says: "If Antarctica is the beating heart of the planet, as I believe it is, it deserves to be cared for with all of our best intentions."

Explore the Issue

1. **Explain** According to Bowermaster, why is it important to keep a close watch on Antarctica's climate?

2. **Draw Conclusions** Why should climate change in Antarctica matter to the rest of the world?

Plant a Tree
—and report your results

You don't have to explore the oceans to fight climate change. You might start by cutting down on your use of fossil fuel energy. You've also learned that trees help reduce the amount of carbon dioxide in the atmosphere. By planting trees in your community, you can make a difference.

IDENTIFY

- Find out about tree-planting projects in your school or community.

- Invite experts to explain the best kinds of native trees for your climate. Also learn when and how to plant saplings.

- Find a donor source for native trees, and arrange for their delivery.

ORGANIZE

- Advertise your project through school or local media.

- Have volunteers sign up to plant the trees and gather supplies, such as gloves, shovels, water, and mulch, for planting day.

- Schedule volunteers to water the newly planted trees weekly.

Students work together to plant a tree in their community on Arbor Day.

DOCUMENT

- Take before-and-after photos of the site(s) where you plant the trees and photograph the trees during each season.

- Label your trees with signs or make a map of the area that shows the kinds of trees you have planted.

- Keep a log about when and how you care for the trees, and record their growth each month.

SHARE

- Use your photos and recordings to create a multimedia presentation about your tree-planting project and share it with your class.

- Create a blog about your project from planning to planting and follow-up. Include information about trees and climate change.

- Encourage others to plant trees by creating a visual display of your project for your local library or community center.

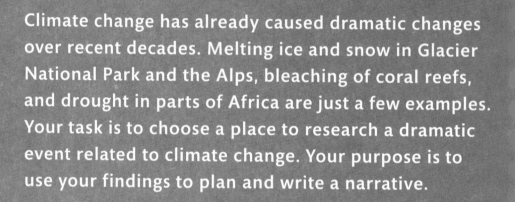

Write a Narrative

Climate change has already caused dramatic changes over recent decades. Melting ice and snow in Glacier National Park and the Alps, bleaching of coral reefs, and drought in parts of Africa are just a few examples. Your task is to choose a place to research a dramatic event related to climate change. Your purpose is to use your findings to plan and write a narrative.

RESEARCH

Use the Internet, books, and articles to find the following information:
- What was the climate like in the early 1900s?
- How has the climate changed over time?
- What dramatic natural events occurred, and how are they related to climate change?

As you research, be sure to take notes and keep track of your sources.

DRAFT

Review your notes about the location you chose. Then select one climate event to dramatize in your story.

- Begin by describing the event's setting with vivid details that will engage the reader.
- Narrate the story through the eyes of a person or an animal. Establish and maintain a consistent point of view, and provide the context for your story.
- The middle paragraphs should present the sequence of events that led to the changes. Use precise words and sensory language to describe them. Use helpful transitions to convey sequence.
- In the final paragraph, wrap up the story in a way that makes the reader want to learn more.

REVISE & EDIT

Read your first draft to make sure that it clearly tells the story of how climate change affected one place in time.

- Does the beginning get the attention of your audience and introduce the topic and setting?
- Does the body of the story present a logical sequence of events and include descriptive details?
- Does the ending flow from the story in a reflective, thought-provoking way?

Revise the narrative to make sure it is clear and complete. Then check your paper for errors in grammar, spelling, and punctuation.

PUBLISH & PRESENT

Now you are ready to publish and present your narrative. Print out your narrative, or write a clean copy by hand. Consider adding photos or graphics to enhance the text. Publish your narrative in a class magazine or Web site.

Visual GLOSSARY

aquifer *n.*, a layer of underground rock that contains water

atoll *n.*, a ring-shaped reef or island made of coral

biofuel *n.*, a renewable energy source made from organic materials

climate change *n.*, a long-term change in average weather conditions on Earth

deforestation *n.*, the process of cutting and clearing trees for fuel or farmland

fossil fuel *n.*, a carbon-based energy source formed in the earth

global warming *n.*, a rise in the average temperature near Earth's surface

greenhouse gas (GHG) *n.*, a chemical compound released into the atmosphere where it traps heat near Earth's surface

ice shelf *n.*, a platform of ice that extends from the shore into the ocean

infrastructure *n.*, public works systems

mangrove *n.*, a tropical saltwater plant that forms a dense mass of supporting roots

renewable energy *n.*, a natural power source that does not harm the environment

sustainability *n.*, land management that preserves ecological balance and natural resources

atoll

mangrove

deforestation

sustainability

renewable energy

INDEX

SKILLS